In *Swimming to Alaska*, Doris Jean Lynch writes of something "electric, energized, waiting for me to pick up the pen and sing," and that is what these poems do: Sing—they celebrate life's fullness. Here are poems that demonstrate an understanding of the importance of place and physicality that is balanced with an appreciation of whimsy and the mystery that surpasses the physical.

The collection opens with intimate and autobiographical poems set in Alaska when Lynch was a young mother and ends with an eye toward the human collective, the surreal and esoteric, with hints at a possible apocalyptic end for our imperiled planet. Lynch takes us on a voyage, not only geographically through her evocative haibun, but to other times and lives through her persona poems in such voices as poet Emily Dickinson, artist René Magritte, astronomer Maria Mitchell, and Antarctic explorer Robert Falcon Scott.

Woven throughout are poems that delight in exploring polarity: an encounter that is both nightmare and exultation, the visceral needs of the body in concert with the gossamer nudges of the spirit, an abiding love of the "needle-rush of stars dazzling" as well as the darkness that makes them manifest to human eyes. Lynch deftly traverses and unifies these polarities through an impassioned attention to detail—images, textures, sounds, smells. Fundamental to it all is the polyphony of life and death. Here are poems that awaken us to the sheer miracle of being alive.

—Nancy Chen Long, author of *Wider than the Sky*.

Other Works By Doris Jean Lynch

Meteor Hound, MediaJazz.com, 2023

Praising Invisible Birds, Finishing Line Press, 2008

J.R.R. Tolkien: Creator of Languages and Legends,
Franklin Watts, 2003

Swimming to Alaska

Poems

Doris Jean Lynch

Bottom Dog Press
Harmony Series

Huron, Ohio

Bottom Dog Press, Inc.
PO Box 425, Huron, OH 44839
Lsmithdog@aol.com
http://smithdocs.net

CREDITS:
Co-Editors: Larry Smith, Susanna Sharp-Schwacke
Cover & Layout Design: Susanna Sharp-Schwacke
Cover Art: Thom Gillespie

TABLE OF CONTENTS

Dedication

To Thom, Kristen, Cody, and David, adventurers all!

.

SECTION I

The earth, at its core, is winter; the universe is winter...
Winter waits and finds all life.

—Richard Nelson

FIRST CALL, CODY
Kivalina, Alaska

Was it the evening Oscar
drove past with his dog team?
When we heard the whoosh of his sled
over the crusted snow? Or perhaps,
the night the stove oil ran out
and our cabin turned as black as though
the engine of the world had blown out.

Surely, a night when the aurora borealis
rippled her flaming chest across the sky,
and we lay in each other's arms listening to
the angels soldering heaven. Or perhaps a night
more ordinary when the iron stove spat
sparks across the floorboards and Orion
spilled its tallow over the sky. A night when
lemmings squeezed their swag-bellied bodies
under our door leaving tiny
prints on the shed counters.

That night, you little darling, were cruising along
at just the right longitude, just the right latitude
through the cosmic dust. How lucky we were
to be billeted just north of the Arctic Circle
waiting, waiting.

Your sister slept soundly, her hands
clutching *Goodnight Moon* while I called
to you with my belly and breasts. Outside,
our chimney, all the village chimneys
poured clouds into the sky, little
grey ghosts beckoning you home.

Night Visitor
Juneau, Alaska

Once in Alaska I slept
in a forest on a mountaintop
on a night with no moon.
During the night, a bear came
down and sniffed at my face.

Part of me thought
this is a nightmare, another
part rejoiced, "Isn't it grand
to be finally, wholly animal?"
Another part of me held my breath
as though my breath
were the one pulse a bear
might recognize in the hemlock forest.
Inside my sleeping bag
I pulled my breasts
toward my spine. My baby
still nursed and I hoped
that the bear would not maul
me for the taste of my milk.

Yet, when that burly
wall of night leaned
over my face, I understood
how the grass feels
when rain starts to fall:
unprotected, vulnerable,
yet eagerly seeking
the wet brush of life.

Swimming to Alaska

We travel through Oregon and Washington. In British Columbia, the Fraser River pounds beside the highway, spinning clouds of mist into the air. Roadside signs advertise fresh apricots. They taste like the northern air, fresh and delicious. Just past Edmonton, we turn onto the Alaska-Canadian Highway.

Every day we take side trips to lakes. I dive into them, relishing the silky feel of the water. At each water's edge I imbibe deep breaths, then dive as deep as I dare—until my lungs ache, and I surface again, desperate for air. Locals greet us as if we are neighbors. Children approach and ask our names.

After driving for hours in almost continual daylight, we rush down the banks of wild rivers, finding quiet eddies where we ride currents safely downstream. At Liard Hot Springs, we arrive just after a grizzly has cleared the pools. I lower my head under the spring's black liquid.. The only person that stayed after the bear sighting yells excitedly, "Don't stay under! Bruin may return searching for cooked meat."

Crossing into Alaska, on the highway to Tok, we see signs for another lake. A boulder-rimmed cirque. For the first time I have to force myself to jump in—the air temperature has dropped considerably. Once inside, I feel I can stay forever. My skin adjusts to the cold swirling around me. My heart's rapid beat begins to slow. The water becomes liquid skin.

Two weeks later, we fly to Nome. At a beach by the Bering Sea, the Inupiat kids race over the sand in in gym shorts, dungarees, flowered dresses, t-shirts advertising California Fried Chicken. No one owns a bathing suit. I dive under the waves, then leap up sputtering. Droplets of frigid water splatter over my arms and thighs. I spear my body into another crest realizing that this will be the last swim of the year because, here, south of the Arctic Circle, it is already fall with winter barreling right behind.

dogpaddling
the Bering Sea
searching for Asia

FEEDING AN ORPHAN REINDEER FAWN

First, know it's the sorrow
in her eyes that you are feeding.
Then cover your arm with
the soft stubbed hair of the doe.
Fill a baby bottle with formula,
Land O' Lakes, or you can make
your own. Here's a recipe:
26 ounces evaporated milk,
2 generous ounces cod liver oil,
fresh egg if available.

Now, most importantly,
cup your furred hand
over the chin of the fawn,
and with that deer-wooed arm
pour your love into the calf
until your love ignites rivers
of moonlight in her eyes.

Lastly, never forget:
take a warm damp rag,
press it close against
the buttocks. Do this the first
week or two until she learns
to pass her manure easily,
until it comes dancing out
of the folds of her skin.
The orphan will bond
with you then, buck the fates
of the universe for your love.

Village Mail Plane

We zoom down the Kotzebue runway: my husband, toddler, and I. Seconds before the Cessna dives into the Chukchi, the plane jerks skyward. The pilot turns north.

Behind us, he's jammed mailbags, boxes, and a dozen, twenty-quart plastic containers filled with God knows what. After ten minutes, we see no sign of life below: no roads or cabins. No winding lines of caribou, or solitary bears fattening up before snow covers the tundra. Only the placid sea to our left, and the Brooks Range to our right.

Kristen babbles in my lap; she hums to the engines' roar. Gazing outside the window, I notice gnashed rocks below. Although only August, the snow extends halfway down the mountains. If we're forced to emergency land, we're goners in this land barely touched by humans.

As the plane's motors stutter and nearly stall, I hug Kristen tighter. The pilot yells something unintelligible; his headphones make conversation impossible. When he turns and notices my terrified face, he gives a thumbs-up.

Soon, a barrier island appears next to the coast. The pilot eases into a slow dive. Round and round we descend toward a small village on a narrow peninsula. Kivalina, our new home.

walking the tundra
feeling the planet's wobble
with each step

AUGUST NIGHT BEYOND THE GLACIER
Juneau, Alaska

In Mendenhall Valley we sense
the dark shapes of horses
in the night, smell their dung
and the sweet promise of hay.

Stars revolve in the heavens
close enough to caress and a sliver
of moon gives us hunger, but
the whole night is about hunger:

the way wind off the icefields
erupts stars on our naked
flesh, the way the light of stars
pulses through our blood.

The way you eclipse the celestial
beings by climbing on top of me,
borrowing their fire. The way coyotes
claim night once, twice, thrice.

And the way the aurora borealis
shakes her wide sky-blanket
of viridian and red.
How love is like that night

light-filled and primal, and how
longing prods the horses
into the northern fields
to graze and graze until dawn.

WHALE'S GIFT
Juneau, Alaska

It's two and a half days since Cody's birth. He was born just before midnight, after a four-hour labor, only slowed by the umbilical cord lassoing around his neck. "Stop! Pant! Don't push!" The midwife's commands filled me with terror. Before I knew what was happening, she'd fixed the problem with a slash of her knife.

My energy's back, and I'm revved for a walk. Cody nestles on my chest in a blue front pack. Kris, two and a half, varies between toddling and racing ahead. I feel all jiggly inside. I squeeze my ab muscles tight, convinced that any second I will plop a body part onto Calhoun Street. Perhaps by the governor's mansion. My pace slows.

mist swirls on the mountains   snow-flocked spruce

Gentle rain. My Gortex jacket stretches around my belly, but the zipper refuses any upward progress toward Cody's head, now covered in a bright pink cap knitted by his grandmother, who longed for another granddaughter after birthing four sons. By the pedestrian bridge to the grade school, we stop and rest. I'm already winded even though, less than a week ago, I'd hiked Perseverance Trail despite the nervous stares of fellow hikers and one man's comment, "Yell like hell if anything happens. I'm a pro at CPR!"

We reach Main Street and Tom links elbows. It's super steep from this point down to the wharf. I grit my teeth thinking maybe I should have suggested a shorter stroll. But no, I promised Kris a view of Gastineau Channel and its fisherfolk, possibly reeling in a huge halibut.

Half of forever later, we arrive. Claim the entire wharf. "Nobody fish-eth," Kris says, but she's not disappointed. She points to the town across the channel. "Douglas," she says gleefully, "all lighted up." Through the grey mist, over the grey water, we spot holiday lights. Suddenly, a huge splash sounds.

17

"What—" I start, then simultaneously, Tom and I yell, "Look, Krissy, a humpback!"

We've only seen them while riding the Alaska Marine Highway on the Inside Passage, never in this channel. The mother animal is magnificent, rising and splashing down hard. As though sensing the excitement, Cody stirs in his pack. His head pops up, though it faces me, not this arm of the Pacific. The rest of us scream as we notice a baby whale on the mother's right flank, another on her left. "The Mama whale's brought her babies to meet you, Cody. Bless you into life."

bald eagle
alights on a lamppost
a sound like bells

SEASON OF SNOW AND MILK
Juneau, Alaska

Each January night the snowplow's lights pour through our lace curtains at four, five, even six a.m. As I nurse my son, my finger trails the twin crimson bands on his neck, physical reminders of the umbilical cord that the midwife had to cut to ease his passage into this world.

The night remains quiet except for a plow scraping Calhoun Street before unloading snow into Gastineau Channel. The driver, the baby, and I seem to be the only ones awake in this white world.

At one hundred and seventy-nine inches, the year's snowfall breaks records. As the weeks pass, Cody's clenched body stretches out, his skin loses its post-birth carmine.

We exist outside of time. No moon, no stars, only white flurries float before the plow's headlights. In the next room, my husband and daughter sleep, leaving an empty spot on the family bed.

at daylight
tiny fingers strum my breast—
alpine glow

Conjuring Borealis

Outside your gabled window, wind
unravels the slender petioles of leaves
and trees heavy with fruit balance
over goldenrod pastures.

"My neighbors no longer drink from
my cups," you say. "Why do people
believe cancer is contagious?"

Even thousands of miles away
I cannot let you go. These mountains,
numerous as Pennsylvania fence posts
if only I could mold their firmness,
make whole again those apples upon your chest.

Later when night bandages the sky
under layers of black gauze delicate
as bridal lace, I will bundle up fire
and magic, scrape this Northern
sky clean of its borealis skin and bring
you suitcased in the luggage bins
of airplanes this spray of night sky
to lighten your journey.

November Sky

String of cloud days
oyster-shell grey.
Wake to darkness, breakfast
through half-light.

Season of deer rut,
of crimson seeping
under autumn leaves.
Season of loss, of no
certain tomorrow.

Far across night's
border, geese honk.
How can they fly
with such end-of-day
energy, wings negotiate
such late arrivals?

Yellow disc
will arrive again,
so radiant and ordinary,
and we will give thanks

for one more
perfect day,
no matter how
insect-wing fragile.

Funeral Under the Raven
Inupiat Graveyard, Kivalina, Alaska

All night they built fires
so that this morning their shovels
would slip inside the permafrost,
pickaxes unlocking the frozen earth.

We gather in the field near the airstrip.
The minister steps up to the gaping
hole, so much starker here where
snow is the only punctuation, save
for the lone raven elegizing the sky.

Our prayers rise as the smoke rises.
Two men stoke the fire continuously
to keep the ground from freezing
again before the infant corpse
can be wedged inside.

As the villagers sing, my baby wakens,
squirms. She rides *abu,* the same way
this other child rode inside
his mother's parka until just
days ago. Kristen's hand brushes
the back of my neck as a raven caws.

The sea's waves are scalloped in place.
Mysteriously locked, they lack the pulse
to go on. In this grey rind of a December
noon in Kivalina, Alaska, the rising smoke
makes me think of the infant's soul riding
the only squiggles of heat it will ever know.

POST OFFICE BENEFICENCE
Kivalina, Alaska

At the Alaskan post office located in Ethel Swan's living room, I greet the village ladies, who sit cross-legged on the floor sewing mukluks*. "Come," Alice says, "Let's see that little one inside your parka." As the room's warmth surrounds us, Kristen, my toddler, wakes and pokes her head out. I stoop so the ladies can coo to her in Inupiaq. We share news about the weather and animal sightings—Enok spotted a musk ox on the island—if only the channel were frozen already. Ethel's sons return from hunting and head to a side room for butchering.

Before the high desk, where Ethel conducts official business, I ask about our mail. "None today," she says. "Blizzard winds between here and Kotzebue."

She asks me again to spell the name of the state where I come from.

"P-e-n-n-s-y-l-v-a-n-i-a," she repeats. "Nice long name—just like our Inupiaq ones."

Wishing her good night, I zip my coat and head to the *kunicuk* or storm porch. Just as I yank open the heavy outside door, Enok rushes behind me. "Mother said to give you this." I look inside the old pillowcase, open it enough to detect half a caribou leg. "Can't take that," I say. "Too big a gift—"

"Aaka won't want it back," he answers. "Can I carry it home for you?"

"I have the sled." He takes the caribou from me and secures it to the driftwood sled.

Over the snow, I trudge, and salivate thinking of all the recipes I know for soups, stews, and meat casseroles. My husband will be surprised!

wild yapping
of sled dogs
dog constellations shine

*mukluks: extremely warm boots made from caribou skin turned inside out.

EATING INUPIAQ-STYLE

Whale oil donuts—
white men's flour
spiced with aromas
of the wild sea.

Frozen *kuak*
raw meat sliced from
caribou's rump, buried
all fall in permafrost.

My journey from beansprout-
loving vegetarian to savorer
of moose-meat, caribou-belly,
and last summer's willow leaves
tempered by seal oil, called *serak*.

Underground, the leaves' summer green
alters to a purple black.
Vitamin C bursts on the palate.
Finally, *akutaq**, the highlight

of every feast, gallons of whipped
Crisco, berry-bled, sugar-sweetened.
One taste too much. Preceded by
uuġaq•, jigged for all winter

by the village ladies
in the frigid dark, waiting for life
to quicken under the frozen lagoon
as new life quickens inside me.

Ruthlessly, slamming fish heads
against the ice. Watching them freeze
instantly in minus forty air.
Simmered for hours, we eat heads

24

and my favorite—*paniqtak*,
wrinkled ebony in a jar. To chew
this leathery seal meat preserved in oil
is to taste the sea's sweet navel.

For our final feast in May
our neighbors bring out
muktuk, outer fat of whale,
the pinnacle of Inupiat cuisine.

But, after the meal, my fetus
kicks for the first time.
Since kindergarten, he's chosen
the vegetarian path.

akutaq: arctic ice cream, usually made these days from vegetable short-
ening, berries, sugar and loose snow.
•*uugaq*: arctic cod, an abundant fish in Northern coastal Alaska. They
are often caught by ice-fishing.

ICE FISHING ON THANKSGIVING EVE
Kivalina, Alaska

On frozen snow's rippled palette, a circle of Inupiaq women stoop, then sit cross-legged on the ice. Recently arrived from the Lower 48, I know nothing of winter's immense want. As our jigging unlocks tomcod from the frozen lagoon the women sing century-old songs. Under the ice, hungry fish dart after silver lures. With an awl, a high school girl stabs opens the holes whenever their wide eyes freeze again. I wonder how quickly before the sea ice will fail, whales hunger, fish stocks decline. For now, an incoming tide rushes the fish through a channel that connects the Chukchi to the lagoon. Under a wan sun, we smack each cod onto the ice, where it flash freezes before the great heating that will kill us all.

the sharp stab of capture hook throat eye

THANKSGIVING IN THE INUPIAQ VILLAGE
Kivalina, Alaska

I. Morning
First the sky, delicate as blue crystal
stretched taut over this snowy world.
Snow pellets, the size and texture of sand,
mark the frozen lagoon's skin. Village
women lean forward on plastic lawn chairs,
their legs splayed out over drilled holes.
They jig fishing lines, stack piles of white fish
on top of the snow. Their mittens, made
from wolverine fur, look wide as the sky.

II. Afternoon
All two hundred and twenty of us gather
in the school gymnasium. We balance
dishes on our arms, Inupiaq delicacies:
oogruk (leathery, bearded seal),
muktuk, ptarmigan soup, caribou stew, arctic
ice cream. At the end of the feast, Leonard,
a village elder, calls Enok, Laurie, and Nokton
up to the stage. He congratulates them on their first trout
caught, first rabbit snared, first ptarmigan slingshotted
down from the dwarf willow tree. We honor
these children who have become hunters and also
give thanks to the animal spirits which have
sacrificed their lives for us.

III. Night

Outside, the unusually still Arctic air
lullabies the sea into a cradle of rime.
Inside, native drums pound out the rhythms
of the missing tide. We sink our bodies
into a knee-bent stance, raise and sashay
our arms, dance the dance the Inupiat
have danced for thousands of years,
while above us the aurora borealis
ripples the sky with florets of flame.

Inside, sheltered in each other's arms,
we jig an orphaned Virginia Reel. And though
we can't hear it, the aurora borealis rings
out its bells, such soft tintinnabulations
of longing. We wait for the slow surcease
of the sun, for the days to slip into a great
darkness which even this holiday night
we fear rather than praise.

In the Darkness, Dancing

New Year's Eve in Kivalina, Alaska, eighty miles north of the Arctic Circle. All two hundred villagers gather in the small community hall. We squeeze close, jean-covered thighs and *mukluk*-clad feet touching. No chairs in sight, just a wooden bench for three of Kivalina's oldest and frailest, whom I've seen only once before at a funeral.

We share a feast: caribou soup, raw fish, *paniqtak*, sourdough bread, berry pie, and arctic ice cream (don't ask for the ingredients). Then the final night of Arctic Winter Games begins–tests of endurance that the Inupiat have shared in this dark season for thousands of years. Most strange and taxing of the games is the knuckle walk, in which young men maneuver across the floor holding themselves in a plank position, balanced on only their knuckles and toes. Each round, they leave in their wake oblong-shaped spots of blood on the cement floor.

At midnight, the village leaders clear a spot in the room's center and a few older women begin Inupiaq dancing. The drumming, the women's graceful folding and unfolding of arms and bending and swaying of legs nearly lull me to sleep until Oscar Swan, one of the village leaders, calls out, "Time for the Virginia Reel."

Leaping up, we join the crowd moving across the floor. We strut four steps forward and four steps back, approach each other and turn, do-si-do, reel, gallop up and down the line, duck gracefully under other couples' arch-connected arms, then separate and race down the line. 1 o'clock, 2 o'clock, 3 o'clock: we dance until our faces turn crimson and drip with sweat. By 5 o'clock my woolen socks sport holes. Still, we continue twirling and promenading for another hour until blisters poke from my heels. Finally, Oscar calls the new year officially welcomed. Avoiding hummocks of sled dogs curled under snow, we head home through the dark. It will be hours before a grey sunless dusk wakens our world.

together hearts pound
on the high homemade bed —
Inupiat drums

APPRENTICESHIP FOR THE WALKING LIFE

Did you learn to love hiking
on those long tundra walks when I carried
you cocooned inside my parka, the one
you wear now on polar vortex nights?
We rambled over the frozen lagoon,
then past the singing Wulik. Together,
we traversed the hummocky waves
of Alaska's permafrosted tundra.

Sometimes, I sang but mostly my Sorels
sawed through the snow, a sound similar
to tuning an old tuba. Nights came early,
at two in the afternoon, a pale, *ulu**-shaped
moon rose. Riding *abu•*, your world was
primarily sound then: ptarmigans hurdled
into flight; a snowy owl mewed being chained
to an old log, one that had ridden
the sea currents all the way from Siberia.

Now I walk Griffy Lake's trails, cross
fallow fields, pace beside the endless
railroad tracks. Car lights point and shoot,
and once or twice a year, a pale aurora
hangs over our subdivision. Sometimes snow
floats down, sometimes moths bat against the light,
and in spring, magnolias shed your favorite blossoms.

Keep walking, daughter, over the fallow flanks
of your college town, seemingly as far from me as the stars
that sketch animal shapes across the curve of night.
Be comforted for the stars, although distant burn
bright, and this same sky stretches over the arctic world,
the world you left behind before you realized
you were speaking two languages, English and Inupiaq.
Before memory photographed any of this for you:
frazil°, shuga□, the aurora borealis, before you realized
we were two separate beings going our separate ways.

ulu: a short-handed knife often made from old saws used to cut frozen
meat or fish.
•*abu*: an Inupiaq word for carrying a baby inside a parka for warmth.
°frazil: ice that is a kind of slush.
□shuga: white chunks of ice that form from slush churned by moving
seawater.

First Plane to Point Hope
After a painting by Kivetoruk Moses, 1968

We have eaten the quivering *muktuk*
of a freshly killed bowhead

and watched the night sky tremor
with red and green flames.

But this is something new:
a giant whining insect

bisecting clouds and flying
over the Chukchi toward us.

Caleb leaps up in the umiak's bow
and points skyward, abandoned by all

Inupiaq words. Etok and Charley
bend low, bodies curled into waves.

From them comes a mysterious
keening—a sound our people wailed

only when tragedy struck before
we were blessed with Christian

prayer. From side to side in the bow,
Abel's dog paces, clanging its chain.

The bell-like sounds seem to compel
the huge two-winged creature closer.

Our eyes lock on Point Hope's rocky promontory
as I steer the umiak diagonal to land, heaving

all my fear into paddling, knowing that
our lives depend upon me remaining calm.

Suddenly all in the boat—Abel, Caleb, Enok
and I—suck in our breaths as the creature

pauses directly over us, circling
once before descending. We see

a human inside, or is it a god? Human
enough, Caleb says lifting his eyebrows,

to give us a wave. Later, we radio
Barrow and discover that this strange

new flying machine is called a biplane,
but only after we teach ourselves

how to walk on the world again.

Leaving Kivalina

We arrived in Kivalina
like people fallen from a star
just two months after arriving in Alaska.
Now it's time to depart, to leave
this land of ice-tundra, trumpeter
swans, snow geese. This narrow peninsula
bumped by frazil, shuga, a thousand
kinds of sea ice. This land where
the aurora borealis rings out prayers
in timpani of sound.

We share our last meal at the Adams' place
next door: Pilot bread, bowls brimming
with seal oil. Angeline serves whale liver, a treat
from the cousins in Point Hope. All through the meal,
the mail plane from Kotzebue buzzes on the edge
of consciousness. Even before we're finished,
Caleb's three-wheeler roars to the door, we jump
into its storage cart. Goodbyes are quick, muted.
We plan to return again in the fall but never do.

We soar over the black ravens,
the Californian-style houses
planted so far north, the village
school with its full-size gymnasium,
Kivalina's two small churches, one Quaker and
one Episcopal from the days white ministers
assigned each village two Christian denominations.

We fly over the sea with its open leads,
the entrance to the lagoon with its black meltwater roiling.
Already, the late May sun has scraped the tundra boulders
free of snow. We rise higher and higher
until the barrier island becomes a small,
white arm, until Kivalina's houses
shrink into tiny matchboxes and the village
itself becomes as small and perfect
as my two-year-old's hand.

Section II

Cold in the earth, and the deep snow piled above thee!
— Emily Bronte

FEBRUARY ICE STORM

Eighty-four years ago, your first birthday—
another century, another world.
Horse carts clattered over cobblestones,
fruit & vegetable men yodeled to housewives,
urging them to buy. Down Philadelphia's
Allegheny Avenue, flappers wove, sequined
dresses competing with stars. Sinister
fox faces draped ivory necks.

Another February, you lie
cocooned in a hospital bed
in Crystal River's ER across
from the twin-headed nuclear plant
that buttresses the Gulf of Mexico.
A phone call away, Indiana hail hisses,
and trucks disgorge salt onto Highway 45.

There is no safety for any of us
in this life: not drivers skidding
from amber stripe to bike lane,
not doctors carefully scanning
your MRI, not our black lab sprawled,
legs akimbo on the glazed lawn
as a lone cardinal seeks shelter
under the crystalline hedge.

Ice comes from that mysterious place;
none of us can see through or beyond.
But isn't it enough when the clouds
make music? When we tilt our faces
upward and our mouths open like those
of baby starlings, inviting tiny pellets
to enter and melt on our tongues.

First Snow After Your Death

How does snow sound from below,
no longer marked by your boot prints?

Can you still hear rustling—half wind,
half crystals scraping against each other?

Is your mouth still turned away
as though from a kiss?

How indiscriminately snow hides
everything: pond, furrows, copses, boulders.

Later, we'll offer you clods to breathe, and
irrigate your thirst with rain and snowmelt.

After blizzard's blast, we'll search for you,
leaving our cursive prayers on top of the snow.

WALKING IN THE QUAKER WOOD

I wanted to tell you about the fox:
how it paused on a hillock of snow,
the tall pines of the Quaker wood standing
sentinel around it, a watchful army of trees.
As I stared, the fox's head jerked upward,
as though someone had wrenched a rope
on its neck toward the sky. Following
its direction, I caught the last split-second
of a shooting star's odyssey down
to Earth. It streaked across the sky before
disappearing into the haze of man-made lights.

I raced back to your room to tell you
that I recognized your soul inside
the fox's sleek body, your muscles
rippling its fur. I rushed into the house
through the storm-door that sang
on its hinges, up the stairs to your room,
not stopping until I found you
on your bed, not stopping until I felt
the rise and fall of your breath
on my palm. I stood listening to you
the way I listened to my children breathe
when they were new, two fingers poised
under their nostrils in the dark.

I held your hand, its veins
blue as the sky at first
starlight. I wanted to tell you
about the fox, how her prints
scrimshawed the snow, how the
night came alive with her breath,
how, high above us, one star
exploded to dust in the night.

Day of the Dead
Taos, New Mexico

On the Day of the Dead
the electric wires chattered
like starlings when we visited
Kit Carson Cemetery. Someone had left
the black iron gate open. Someone,
maybe the same person, or another
from the dancing costumed mob
had left apples, oranges, and skull
cookies on top of the graves.

Even as the gate creaked in the wind,
as Mabel Dodge Luhan's copy
of *The Pied Piper* rustled its pages
in a come hither way, the dead stuck
to their roots, their quiet passageways.

Perhaps, we partied too loudly
with our whizzing sparklers
or their erratic light hurt
the lonely sockets where
their eyes once stood. Maybe
we danced too hard on their roofs.

Certainly, we did we not show
any fear as we read their names
chiseled on stone, and ignored their bones
changing to humus under piñons' rocky soil.
For whatever reasons, the dead remained
under the earth, and we walked home
lonely for them, having brushed
their names with our candle flames
and the limb-shadowed light of the moon.

On the Way to September

There's an ease to late summer, a fullness. The pampas grass is thick—its contiguous green spikes offering a refuge for squirrels and rabbits. On the far side of the house, the walnut tree has begun its staccato droppings. The sunflowers and tall daisies reach for the sky as the tomato branches curl downward under the weight of heavy fruit. Can old age be like this? This feeling of abundance, of having survived the tornadic winds of spring, the rollicking thunderstorms of July to come to this day full of stillness and the world's beauty.

in the garden
half gold, half green peppers—
how veined your hands

INDIANA, LATE AUGUST

Why do we never remember
moments such as this: the chocolate
lab swimming her snout
through the garden, the rasping calypso
of crickets, grey clouds tumbling over
each other in their mad race to greet Ohio?

Instead we seek what? Epiphanies, hurrahs,
crescendos, not the subtle reach
of the body toward the lowering
sun, the sparrow releasing the day's last song,
and the first frogs welcoming night.

BENEATH THE VOICES OF RAVENS
Pueblo Bonito, Chaco Canyon, New Mexico

We are shadows grasping for shadows of the distant past. Others who walked these paths, sought warmth and camaraderie inside these walls, welcomed newborns, comforted the sick, told stories. The same bright sun warms our backs. We wait as they did for the silence of night, the jeweling of stars, hope for a new dawn.

rising
to the rising sun
Pueblo voices

FAREWELL POEM
China, 810 A.D.

Autumn sky, metal-taut.
Jug wine every evening.
Rhyme games. Who can conjure
a Chrysanthemum Moon?
In the cool morning, geese
barks wake us both.
Last day. Poets must part.
Cut a swath between fields.

Line marked by absence.
Riddled with barley and
twined arms of grain.
Follow the feathered path.
As you scale mountains,
I'm jealous of your climbing legs,
your feet probing rock,
railing against separation.

Your journey of many weeks
ends on the morning of first snow.
At the final crest, you notice
below your wife's ebony hair
swaying over the russet gate,
her hands rescuing a lone
pumpkin shrouded with frost.
How many mountain rivers
now roar between us?

THE WEIGHT OF THE SOUL

To compute it, the unscientific suggest, weigh the body un-clothed shortly before death, then immediately afterward. Never mind the logistics of that. But let's make clear, those few ounces of difference will never bring your mother back. Perhaps, wiser to follow the trajectory of the jazzy 40s song that floats through the ether the moment her soul takes wing. The moment you step outside to welcome the equinox at 2:42 p.m. as vernal breezes cause the flesh-colored tulips to bob, reaching for a sky they will never touch.

gentle lift
of forsythia branches...
skywriting

Furrows

The plowers plowed…they made long their furrows.
Psalm 129:3

Where will I sleep
in the furrows of death?
Will I find a dove willing to pillow
my cheek against its soft down?

If only the patterned grasses
might curry my bare legs and arms.
This burrow, this shaped hummock,
will it provide a clear view of sky?

What of the clouds racing past—
too fleeting for shrouds?
Where will I sleep in the burrows
of death? What will I cling to?

Root, barnacle, rock face? What fearsome worlds
will I enter, unprotected, lacking a guide?
Piercing through hard soil,
how many clods of earth
will block my passage?

Will my body be able
to find its way?
And will this last sleep
provide: sanctuary, shelter?

MISTER HANDSTAND MAN

I remember katydid-patrolled
evenings, when you strutted
up and down the driveway
on your hands. Your feet dusting
the slippers of the Seven Sisters as Venus
poured tallow across the western sky.

You could balance there forever,
pirouette, even improvise a kind
of flamenco dance, as you belted
out the lyrics from "Carmen."

I was proud that you could tap
the clouds with your heels,
proud that you could somersault
out of anything, landing gracefully
on Planet Suburbia again.

Who could have guessed
that you'd catapult out of West Philly's
university ghetto only to land in upstate
New York? Who could have guessed
that you'd perform one last handstand
by the tracks outside Elmira?

Did you press handprints
onto the soft grass? Fling your feet
skyward challenging those gravity-
bound stars? Did you yodel our special
yodel while hovering over the earth
as the train hammered toward you?

If so, why did I hear nothing, nothing
not even the blackberry wind?

SOUND PATINA

The dead listen more
than the living. Camouflaged
in dry cornstalks, they stand
attentive as corpse-soldiers.

At night's hem the disappeared
respond to willows' sway
as fog's scent rises from the belly
of Black Bottom Creek.

The missing tune out frog bellows
and the shrieks of night birds.
In the mix of sounds, they chance upon
lovers' sighs, the laughter of children.

By sea's border, the unborn hide beneath
bleached logs. They wait, they hesitate,
biding this time before time. Beyond,
a canto of waves leaps toward the sky.

Lake Griffy Woods at Winter Solstice

Geese stream across the sky.
I walk through Griffy Woods,
surprised by newly bare branches.
Stalwart beech hands cling
to color despite dunness
all around. I remember
how summer once knit together
these leaves. An egret lifts
her pond-blue body skyward.
Most of my friends live
far away—one dying.
Tell me, who owns
this silence.

SECTION III

The past is a great darkness and filled with echoes.
—Margaret Atwood

In a Montgolfier Over Lyons, France
Elizabeth Thible, June 4, 1784

I.

Seven months after men conquered air
for the first time, I ascended. First woman
to ride the air currents, I accompanied
my friend, the artist, Fleurant. My teapot,
that warm, liquidy heart, rested beside us
next to a half-dozen baguettes wrapped in a baker's
towel. I belted arias as we floated
over the burgundy fields. Jokingly, I told
Fleurant that I was auditioning for God.

II .

The Montgolfier brothers, paper makers
from Annonay who invented hot air balloons,
believed that smoke had a special
property called levity. We sensed
this levity as we rose over the crowds of soldiers,
shopkeepers, and royalty (who rode carriages all the way
from Paris eager for some death-thrill entertainment.)
Under the silk flag-cloth, Fleurant and I
shared a picnic lunch. As we floated over the hills,
our balloon frolicked in zigzags of wind. Far below,
a covey of oaks offered their wide green laps.
Lower still, we noticed people—harmless
stick figures—planted on earth
that although we'd broken free of,
we still wanted to praise
with both motion and song.

PULLING SKY HOME WITH OUR HANDS
René Magritte

One morning a balloon
floated toward us from the blue
hills. We children ran toward it, our hands
raised like leaves, beckoning. What power
coursed through our fingers, as the heavenly
object began to descend, as it lowered still,
until like a great cumulous cloud,
it engulfed our house.

1899, the hinge of a new
century, and the philosopher
(for that's what we called aeronauts then)
climbed out of his wicker nest to discover
where he had landed. "How odd," he explained,
"I never planned a stopover in Gilly."

Mother ran her fingers over the balloon's
silk belly. She envisioned everything
she could make from it: dresses,
pantaloons, curtains, if only
this stranger would relinquish
his unnatural kinship with air.

Thirteen years later, the air machine
was the first thing we thought of when
we found Mother drowned by her own hand
in the Sambre River, a nightdress sheltering
her head, the current frothing in two forks
around her. Her nightgown, the same topaz,
as the philosopher's balloon, but this time
riffled by water instead of air.

RECORDER OF HARMONIES

*My brother would have been very much at a loss but for
my assistance.*
—Caroline Lucretia Herschel, 1750-1848

I've seen the brilliance of stars
up close, stared into the belly of the universe.
How many women can say that? Most nights
I'm content to record Will's discoveries
garnered from long hours gazing through
the telescope he constructed, considered
the eighth wonder of the world.

In Slough, each night my pen races across
paper. I cartograph sky's wonders, translating
brightness and motion into numerals,
converting all into coordinates. In permanent
peacock blue, I draw Will's new map
of the universe with arcs for mysterious orbs
he's discovered while gazing across space.

At breakfast, Cook refuses to believe that
other worlds exist tossed among the pinpricks.
"Sheep on hills don't tumble off, brook salmon
don't fly from sky. Blasphemy!" she mutters,
snapping her towel against flies but slapping
my wrist as though by accident. "God made us this
one perfect world." Harrumphing, she hands me
the smallest serving of plum pudding.

Most nights I love being Will's recorder,
his writing arm. He rescued me from Hanover:
a life of servitude to mother and brothers: cleaning,
darning, cooking. He taught me music, trained me
to be a chamber singer. Imparted the skills by which
I made my living, bringing Handel oratorios
to fancy drawing rooms. Always, he encouraged
me to praise our world with song.

But his astronomy lessons interested me most.
To sing takes body, breath, and spirit, but how
much more inspiring is recording the transit
of heavenly bodies, and discovering the itinerant
paths of comets? When Will climbs down from
his telescope for a smoke at three o'clock, I rush up
and observe the fluttering pulse of Rigel
and the jeweled hoops that grace Saturn's belly.

In 1779, William began his first detailed sweep
of the heavens. I kept nightly logs, and after
two hours of distracted sleep, rose to document
that panoply of planets, their transits, the orbits
of comets. After Cook's begrudging breakfast—
"Missy, I pray for your doubting soul."—I list
sightings of new moons and satellites. Tired as I
am, numbers dart from me fleet as brook trout.

For me the sky itself is music. Each night
revolving orbs create new sonatas. For me the sky
is a lover arched above, enfolding, the husband
mother predicted I'd never have because of my
pox-scarred face. The night sky entices,
composed of both the known and the unknown.
When I record Will's observations—and of late,
my own—I choreograph celestial music.

Will has married now, has other duties.
After his discovery of Uranus, King George III
appointed him Royal Astronomer. Since then,
I've started my own solitary sweep of the night sky,
and discovered twelve new nebulae.
Nights, when Perseid shoots crystalline arrows past
Pollux and Castor, I wonder if men (women too?)
will someday explore the faraway planets.

Sometimes in autumn, I think I've detected
another planet's scent, pine-green
and pear-sweet. Removing my gloves,
I climb down the king's ladder, lift my arms
toward the salted dome above and belt out
arias toward Leonid's cache of stars.

LADY ASTRONOMER

I believe in women, even more than in astronomy.
                                                    –Maria Mitchell

This is the only river I want,
this river of starlight. My dream
is to order the heavens, to catalog the stars.
Not that mystery can be counted, immensity
enumerated. But one can still try to diagram
its contours. When I was a child,
I watched from our widow's walk
the wind-whipped whalers race
out to sea. Landlocked by prejudices
against my sex, I chose to navigate
instead, this sea of stars.

Emily and the Meteorite

Counting loves, I stop at one.
Does anything other than fibrous
muscle compose the heart?
Many deem me a shy recluse.
Others call me fey—who really knows
themselves when young? Amherst neighbors
think I dwell too much on faith, leaving
scant energy to abrade the wound
of my birth, my livelong subservience to men.
No freedom from household chores to write poems
by the apple orchard in daylight. No wooden globe
to spin and plan a solitary tour through Kazakhstan.
Instead, only this ebony rock to conjure
the mysteries of the universe,
this otherworldly stone that
plummeted down through chimera clouds
—a missive from space beyond—whose
inscriptions I'll never decode
but add instead to my own.

Epistolary Moths

In keen and quivering ratio/ to the ecstasy.

—Emily Dickinson

Master, I send you these moths
No, sire, rather your heat will entice
them as the fiery sun draws
alabaster moon in its wake.

If my hands must be caged,
let these wings become
emissaries of want. Slam shut
your lexicon. Bury your ears
against the sibilants of unsatisfied
desire. Tonight, I command these
moths to erupt, to bruise
forever this air.

CALLED TO COMPOSE BY THE DRUMMING BIRD

A black and white, red-beaked
woodpecker taps against my window.
Inside my room I attire myself
in a skirt sewn from the master's letters,
carefully affixing with thread two canceled
postmarked stamps just above the hem.
"Phila" reads one, "delphia" the other.
Tap, tap. A woodpecker frenzies
against the windowpanes.

I embroider several poems
together to make a crown. Barefoot,
I leap across the floorboards. My words
feel too giddy with air. I replace
the poems with an Old Testament
borrowed from Mother's room,
her weak, curled form sleeping,
and strut past the windows
with it balanced perfectly.

The woodpecker favors rotten
shutter-wood. My family knocks
and knocks against the door: Father,
Vinnie, Susan, our sister-in-law
from next door. "I'm sewing," I call out.
"Sorrowing. Studying. Sleeping."

I rest my head against God's ear,
the ivory and golden whelk a family
friend brought me from Provincetown. While resting,
its fleshy ear presses against my hard angular one.
All night, the Atlantic pounds inside my head.
Words rise like moths fluttering in candlelight.
By morning, most have faded—but a residue
remains, electric, energized, waiting for me
to pick up the pen and sing.

TOLSTOY'S LAST QUESTIONS

Snow crystals fell winter after winter,
small white moths, which clung
to your eyelashes and beard.
All your life you studied death
as though it were a science or an art,
questioning how and when
the soul takes leave of the body.

When you could no longer share
the lifestyle of rural luxury
your wife so loved, a way of life
which contradicted your basic beliefs, you decided
to wander. After years of fighting your conscience,
on the morning of October 28, 1910,
you boarded a train, certain that Sofya
or one of her agents would follow. But instead
of keeping your identity secret, you lectured
everyone in the carriage on pacifism and non-violence.

At eighty-two you began a rail journey across Russia.
Your quest: to find a simple, out-of-the-way spot
to end your life, some shack in the taiga*
where you could honor God by swallowing
mush and sleeping on an earthen floor. You coasted
over the rails with no destination in mind
until your body could no more move than those ducks
you shot full of lead as a young man at Yasnaya Polyana.

On that trip through the Russian autumn,
pneumonia struck, bringing you weakness, fever.
The Astapova station master offered his cottage.
There in a simple, working-class room,
you battled your last illness. Earlier you'd instructed
your daughter, Alexandra, and your followers
to record your death. You implored them

to ask these important questions: "Do you see
life as you usually see it? Or has it become
a progression toward love and God?"
So others might learn about death before
it held them in its sway, you requested, "If I should not
have the strength to speak, and the answer
is yes, I shall close my eyes; if no, I shall look up."

But during those last days, your friends faltered.
Aware of your greatness, they prayed for you
instead of seeking answers to tough philosophical
questions. They tried to restore your health
with alcohol rubs, medicines, cups full of comfrey tea.
To remind them, you lifted gnarled fingers but instead
of recognizing your quest, your soul's duty to the living,
to those unborn, they offered mineral water, rare oranges
from Georgia, dried sturgeon. Meanwhile, guards
barred your wife from entering. The countess
had rented her own train and followed you.
"Spare him her madness," one of your
followers said, "her annoying insistence."

Two days later your lips turned blue, your soul
unfettered like a birch leaf in wind. Still no one
asked those important questions. Out of what?
Fear, repulsion, a stilted sense of death-side propriety?

But already it was too late. You discovered that death
was similar to birth, a pulsing toward light, a painful
heaving and sawing into and out of darkness. Outside,
Sofya paced the tracks, a lioness sniffing wind for news
of her mate. Hadn't forty-eight years of arguments
been enough? They interviewed her on film. Instead
of your death teaching the living how to prepare
for their own, it became an international news event.

You left great books, loyal disciples, a proud woman
who refused to break, and this riddle, the riddle of death
unanswered, a language the living can only stumble
against, like moths against a screen
both attracted and repelled by the light.

*taiga: a forest of the cold, subarctic region.

Lost Weekend

A broken tooth,
a cherry pit,
and Tolstoy's Ivan Ilyich—
yes, these three were my weekend.

And yesterday at Sunday breakfast
when the tooth met the cherry pit
and I lost, I spat out part
of my once-living self.

That moment I foresaw
the end, tooth after tooth gone,
my mouth, an open pit,
pink-caverned, and oh,
so full of nothingness,
and Ivan Ilyich with his glasses on,
tossing on his lumpy bed, as his family
played cards in the next room,
laughing and waiting.

WRITING DEATH LETTERS NEAR THE SOUTH POLE
Robert Falcon Scott, Antarctica, March 1912

Dear Kathleen, I write you
this one last time, having failed to be first
conquering the South Pole. Another Antarctic storm
pummels the tent as my Comrades Bowers
and the physician, Wilson, lie in sleeping bags
placidly beside me—having crossed
already to the other side.

I have saved until last this difficult
missive having already notified
my companions' relatives. I praised
their utmost courage to the end, their
tenacity in this cold wilderness
barely accessible to the likes of men.

Dear One, I have lost three hours
in some altered state between being
and non-being. Between gales
and silence, between blasts of wind
and piercings of the deepest cold.
My pencil fell, forcing me to contort
my trunk to pluck it near. Labor gladly done
to rouse myself—must not falter—not before…
Sweet Kathleen, I feel no pain, only sorrow
for abandoning you for my dreams
of glory. But they weren't woven for me
alone, but for our Commonwealth.

Now that I have mentioned the fearsome
gales, a deep, uncanny silence spreads
across the Ross Ice Shelf. How peaceful
the world's countenance seems from this tent
that has sheltered us for weeks—just mere canvas
and the wooden skeleton, Bowers and Wilson
hauled over giant ice pinnacles.

My body slowly turns from this life, fingers
weary from lifting even this light pencil.
Oh, happy thought—I recall that February day
in '02 when I rode bucking *Eva* into the sky,
making weather and geographic observations
from inside our War Department balloon.

In my first trip as aeronaut, I ascended,
reconnoitering with the clouds. Below,
snow undulated in bands of light.
As the basket revolved, I noticed
plateaus, peaks, and angled valleys.
They might have been camouflaged clouds.
So monochrome is the polar palette, it deceives even
the most experienced explorer's eye. Yet, what joy I felt
surveying this ice that has endured for centuries.

Just then the engineer, Skelton, startled us
by releasing the hydrogen from *Eva*.
It was as though Antarctica herself exhaled
a forceful sigh. Tonight, my breath rushes
out as well—heavy and sonorous—a cloud
lingers beneath the tent's wind cloth.
What wonder I felt floating
in the willow basket as I watched a tiny
spot track across the white vastness—
our team hauling the *Discovery's* sledge.

I rejoiced at man's ability to conquer
the difficult elements—air and ice—
for exploration's sake alone. Dear Kate,
while we are still connected—if only
tenuously by this graphite inscribed upon
His Majesty's stationary—hold fast, dear one.
Feel the susurration of circumpolar winds
touching you as I will never again, winds
that whirl toward England, toward you.

Section IV

I often think that the night is more alive and more richly colored than the day.

—Vincent Van Gogh

Taos Sky

How do I describe
this vault of longing?

Sky that makes me want
to lie in a scrubby field all day

and simply observe. Can a human
pay such devoted attention?

For distraction: raspy cottonwood leaves,
sway of chamisa, a magpie's gossipy chatter.

Adding to the sounds, the long-haired builder
pounds his incessant hammer.

The ponderosa pine calls to me with its needles
that patch feathery triangles across a corner of sky.

What more can I want
than this cerulean Heaven?

Only for blue to endure, to grow deeper
until miniscule eyes erupt and weep silver.

Night Swimming

Tonight, I am going to push
the Susquehanna away with my body,
ignore the waning moon's fractioning
of light. Make cuckolds of the night birds
who croon their loneliness until dawn.
Breast stroking to the stridulations
of male crickets, I will shatter
thousands of wavery stars.

NIGHT: SANGRE DE CRISTO MOUNTAINS

Here. Now. Not above,
but mated to earth
through journeys of clarified
light. The Navajo etched
crosses onto rock walls
in Canyon de Chelly
to mark the placement
of stars. Tonight, I watch
one fall. It skips across
Heaven's meadows, close
enough to grasp with my hand,
close enough so that God's fiery
hair singes my heart.

In Liege to the Luminous Spheres

We eat leaves like stars,
there's something galactic
about our hunger.
Each bite of heart leaf,
a jolt to memory; each
chlorophyll sip, a channel
to emerald swards of desire.

Night after night of lightning-strike
fires shatter the canopy, devour
the greenness: spruce, hemlock,
the skinny knives of pine. Indifferently,
stars stare down. With songful
entreaties, we plead to borrow
their celestial powers to prevent
more green from burning.

Count the stars: fifty thousand,
five hundred million, thirty-seven trillion.
When we die the clouds will scan our souls
for empathy before wafting us where?
Andromeda? This life, this porous life entreats
the forests, beseeches the bursting novae, the heavens
surrounding us for belonging, connection, meaning.

Celestial Navigation

To guide by touch
       by tactile brush of stars

Hand to cerebral point
       finger to celestial thigh.

Night equals vacancy of birds,
       needle-rush of stars dazzling.

We rub our eyes before this sky chart
       that maps the Milky Way.

We swim through cosmic seas
       rich with the silt of those who have come before.

Each voyage begins with this
       quick unfurling of sails

This voyage to connect
       with the people-stars of Heaven.

IN THE NORTH WOODS

At bedtime, we eat sky. Curve of August crescent moon, its tiny silver canoe, slices through clouds. Under its shine cicadas thrum, while nearby a blind skunk waddles down the gravel road, rattling stones.

below Orion's belt
a doe and fawn nibble
at shadows

In the dark sky, clouds part and the moon floats past. Night eels swim. Kingfishers dive sharply toward the meadow where we've staked our tent. Hearing a loud shriek, we stare upward, following another night bird's dive. Across the almost dark field, large bushes take on fierce animal shapes. We hear growls in the wind. "Coyote?" you ask. "Wolves, more likely," I answer.

on leaf beds
last season fireflies
pulse faintly

Hey, Moon!

Before I was born, I rolled
you in my diaphanous palms,

but like a bluebird you
soared away from me.

During girlhood I cut you into
pristine wedges, rags to catch

my blood, but you changed into
a rivulet and cascaded away from me.

During sex, I propped you for a pillow,
but my hipbones jutted into your lunar flesh

and you drifted away. When I gave birth,
you duplicated yourself and became

twin mothering breasts, but when I glanced
up, both you and baby were gone.

Now I search the sky each night
for any sign of you, but find only

tiny relics, cold to the touch,
not bright enough for eyes.

When the Stars Beam Music

Stars jiggle in their roosts,
drizzling lemony light over the sea.
Bottom fish greedily imbibe their remnant
energy. Exuding phosphorescence,
they ignore beach reggae and the blasts
of foghorns and motors.

A conch on the beach hums
to the vibration of another universe,
while the surf — sassy and restless

as a white-lipped girl — mantras,
"Come on in." Only the bravest stars do,
with a loud whoosh as they extinguish
their burning selves in the sea.

YOUR LOVE TURNED MY BODY
—After a first line by Nur Jahan

Your love turned my body.
It was headed up the mountain.
Like smoke. Like bear. Like the black arms of crows.

Summer turned the grasses tawny and sun drenched my bare legs.
Each evening when we met, birds and insects wailed.
Your love turned my body.

You taught me what you knew of weather.
The way cumulous clouds eventually yield to rain.
Like smoke. Like bear. Like the black arms of crows.

We met by the river.
Cart wheels yammered over the wooden bridge.
Your love turned my body.

First, we spoke only in words.
Then silently in the language of touch, stroke, and caress.
Like smoke. Like bear. Like the black arms of crows.

But summer ended as you warned that it would.
On a horse cart you drove away into the magenta sun.
Leaving me only sorrow wafting up the mountain.
With smoke. With bear. With the black arms of crows.

ONCE

Once I listened for stars
but heard only electric
wires shriek out garbled music
half cicada screech,
half frog drumming.

Once I reached for your hand,
but it disappeared into a cloud
and began weeping. I tried
to lick the rain off your knuckles,
but it raced away in rivulets of blood.

Once I stood tall on tiptoes
and demanded to talk to God
not any god, but *The* God,
but he had gone home early
that day and never called back.

Now I converse with only
the etched faces of rock,
burnished by wind-shifted
memories as loud-mouthed
magpies cackle and flick
their indigo-blue tails in hurried,
careless goodbyes.

Night Whimsy

What secrets do stars hold
inside their glowing fists?

What silks do redbuds hide
beneath their hidden bells?

Last night's goddess sliced the moon
into an ivory whelk. Unmoored, it floated

across the night sea. Tilt your ear
and hear whales lullaby their young.

In our small garden, I want to imbibe every
green morsel on each spring-leaping tree,

chew every bursting bud. Watch clouds
wrap rigging around the spiral moon.

We can sail there too on tulip-sheathed
boats, faces small as watch-displays,

limbs phosphorescent with longing.

Section V

The outcry of birds, the bullet-whirr of their passing wings, the splashing of water, is, like the falling light, unending.

—Barry Lopez

METAMORPHOSIS AT MIDNIGHT

Step outside tonight and let the darkness enfold you. Stand where you can reach the closest stars and know someday the farthest ones will be yours to cup as well. Romance the rising half-moon. Watch her pearl lantern glow opening the world.

Follow the sawdust path into the woods. Listen. Several voices speak to you, clamor for recognition, response. Let the winds lead you. Don't be swayed by dancing fallen leaves, like any acolyte become as will-o'-the-wisp as they.

See apples on the bough? Experience the fruit's firmness, skin-gloss, rotundity. Think color and stillness; remember breathing can bridge the distance between you. Exude the scent of McIntosh. Command the umbilical stalk to tear and its fruit to fall. As with any meditation, trace your way back; slowly, carefully inhabit your once familiar body.

still sending light   dead stars

In the Wee Hours

Between midnight and dawn, my body practices leaving. Using sheets for sails and the bedframe for a prow, my body rehearses its last goodbye. Stars and moon lose their sway, locked doors no longer contain me, and our bedroom windows become as porous as air.

every quarter hour the cuckoo escapes again

Bird Languages

Before we could speak,
we understood them.
They spoke in riddles: promising
that oak and sycamore would
become ladders to sky, and our tongues—
lost leaves—would attach to
mother-cottonwood again.

While our parents slept in their royal
beds, robins and jays taught us to sing
by whistling, to praise by chortling
sky's blue and gasp of cloud.
From birch and walnut,
they summoned wind until

it soared through our bodies,
poured out of our mouths.
We knew every bird language then:
oriole, thrush, magpie, cluck
of domesticated chicken, even
the hoo-hoo, too-hoo, hoo
of its distant cousin, the barred
owl. We lay in our cribs
listening, practicing.

Ever since we have yearned,
for riddled bark, for stalk's spring,
for vibrating grass and stem,
for morning's fluency of song.

Ecology Is No Passive Noun

They came disguised
in the blades of decapitated weeds.

They came forgetting then erasing
the prayers of their young.

They came with skins turned inside out,
dagger hairs stabbing their burnt limbs.

They came with voices, music, yes, even heart's blood
overpowered by the grinding of machines.

They came bearing the duff of forests in their palms
too small to encircle a hummingbird's heart.

They came —a million, million choruses of canaries—
fluttering wings and shrieking that we must stop

this destruction and ruination of Gaia,
our only home. That we must remember

the earth lives just as we do. That it has
a skin, innards, blood as pure and thick

as our own. That she possesses
no stomach for her own destruction.

CLIMATE GRIEF

In every normal sunset, each tiny rosebud on the deer-amputated bush, every hummingbird's whirl, firefly's blink, even while pulling pennywort and pokeweed from the garden, in each burst of rabbit speed as the tree frog ululates through end-of-summer nights, I marvel at the beauty of this world, sigh deeply for the suffering and die-offs to come.

interregnum
between thunderstorms
mourning doves mourn

BETTER CLOUD'S COUSIN, SHADOW

Pray heaven
won't brim with light,
for I want darkness
to camouflage
eternity's
endless view.

For what calms
more completely
than shadow? What
soothes more
than ebony rising
from the darkening
earth?

Darkness which calls
to our penumbral selves
saying remember
I was your
ether in utero,
your cloud sky,
your cellar,
your scatter, your sow,
your under the earth,
your to and fro.

TOURISTS OF A COLD APOCALYPSE

We decide to travel to the massive ice floes. To stand above them on a high plateau. To feel the land shiver and quake beneath us. To feel in our bodies ice skyscrapers penetrate the continental shelf itself. Like birds flying to a place of abundance, the pull of migration works its power upon us. As we approach, the wind becomes more than wind. It becomes turbulent, an unending cacophony. We reach for each other, hang on with all our strength. We welcome the other abandoned ones: lost children, a pair of frail old ones to burrow between us. Before the rising, slashing Atlantic, we become one, one block of shivering humanity finally seeing our real enemy. In the sheen of ice, we see ourselves: small, mutable, mouths open, begging for forgiveness, mercy.

THE ARKLESS WORLD

The night the rain created great chaos,
it poured into our pockets, puffed out

our blouses and shirts, heaved us into the flood.
Tasting its alluvial waters, energy soared down

our throats, revved our blood. The rushing waters
spoke with women's voices—guttural and fierce.

Was it our mothers and grandmothers wailing?
Or the voice of Eve herself coursing through our veins?

When we begged the water to spare us
its whirlpools and overflowing gullies, the river

forked away from our houses and fields,
claiming its independence. After every black torrent

disappeared and we had no springs or streams,
we chanted and urged it to return, but not one

droplet of fog hung over our town, our country,
our continent. Take what nurtures you, we pleaded:

whether plain, savannah or mountain.
Pluck, when you must, even some

of our bodies. For without you, we are nothing
but dried planks, the filigrees of fallen bees.

What the Dead Miss Most

What the dead miss most
is birdsong, joy shaking down
from the trees, the way grass spreads
its green hair over the graves, and lightning
bugs rise in its shadowy furls switching
miniature yellow bulbs on and off
in the honeysuckle-scented air.

And the frogs, what other creature knows
so much about love madness? Hear them
thrumming loudly in the bulrushes
next to the creek. Remember
how your flesh rose belly
to belly when greeting your love.

When a woman pauses to watch
a hummingbird drink from a flower,
the dead can only guess what has
caught her eye. For what do the dead
remember but the world of the senses?
The smell of freshly mown grass,
a mockingbird mocking, crickets
rustling their prayerbooks, the fog
horn blasting its double note.

During moments such as these,
the dead struggle to leash
in their bones, especially muzzling
that empty spot just above the jaw
where the mouth once lay, pink,
round, and perfect. How painful
to hold back those *ahs* which long
to escape each time a star
splinters its body across the sky.

ACKNOWLEDGMENTS

"Apprenticeship for the Walking Life" *Flying Island*, Nov. 2021. "August Night Beyond the Glacier" *Tipton Poetry Review*, Summer, 2021. "Beneath the Voices of Ravens" *Frogpond*, Vol. 42:2, Summer, 2019. "Better Cloud's Cousin, Shadow" *A Linen Weave of Bloomington Poets*, Lexington, KY, Wind Press, 2002. "Bird Languages" *Commonweal*, Nov. 7, 2008. "Climate Grief" *Contemporary Haibun Online*, 17.3, Dec. 2021. "Conjuring Borealis" *Aurora: 13 Poets on the Aurora Borealis*, Bull Thistle Press, 1991. "Eating Inupiaq-Style" *Tattoo Highway* 19, Winter/Spring 2009. "February Ice Storm" *Flying Island*, Feb. 6, 2017. "Feeding an Orphan Reindeer Fawn" *The Sky's Own Light: Poems from Alaska*, Minotaur Press, 1990. "First Call, Cody" *Quill & Parchment*, May 2014. "Funeral Under the Raven" *Exit 13*, Number Six, 1994. "Hey, Moon!" *Flying Island*, March 5, 2020. "The Hours Between Midnight and Morning" *Tipton Poetry Journal*, 51, Winter, 2022. "Ice Fishing on Thanksgiving Eve" *Contemporary Haibun Online*, Dec. 2022. "In a Montgolfier Over Lyons, France" *River Styx*, No. 50, Fall 1997. "In the Darkness Dancing" *Contemporary Haibun Online*, Vol. 12, No. 3, Oct. 2016. "In the Wee Hours" *Frogpond*, 39:3, 2016. "Indiana, Late August" Spring 2001, Bloomington Transit Poetry Project. "Lady Astronomer" *Confluence*, Vol. 7, 1996. "Metamorphosis at Midnight" *Contemporary Haibun Online*, Dec. 2022. "Night: Sangre de Cristo Mountains" *Flying Island*, Aug. 20, 2018. "Night Swimming" *CALYX* Vol. 34:1, Fall, 2023. "Night Whimsy" *Bitter Oleander*, Vol. 14, No. 2, Oct. 2008. "On the Way to September" *Haibun Today*, Vol. 8, No. 1, March 2014. "Post Office Beneficence" *Haibun Today*, Vol. 13, No. 3, September 2019. "Praising Invisible Birds" *Negative Capability*, Vol. X, No. 1, 1990. "Season of Snow and Milk" *From the Cottage of Visions: Genjuan Haibun Contest: Decorated Works 2015-2017*, Hailstone Haiku Publications, 2018. "Sound Patina" appeared as "Night Sounds" in *The Adirondack Review*, Vol. X, No. 3, Spring 2010. "Swimming to Alaska" *Lynx*: XXVII: 1, February 2012. "Thanksgiving in the Inupiaq Village" *Explorations 1997*. "Tolstoy's Last Questions" *Madison Review*, Vol. 13, No. 2, 1991. "Tourists of a Cold Apocalypse" *Drifting Sands Hai-*

bun, Issue 18, 2022. "The Weight of the Soul" *Frogpond*, 45:3, 2022. "What the Dead Miss Most" *It's All the Rage: Poems About Suicide and Its Alternatives*. Hartford, Connecticut: Andrew Mountain Press, 1997. "Your Love Turned My Body" *Artful Dodge*, Vol. 32/33, Winter 1998.

The following poems were reprinted in *Meteor Hound*, Media-Jazz.com, 2023: "Night: Sangre de Cristo Mountains" appeared as "Beneath the Sangre de Cristo Mountains," "Climate Grief," "Ice Fishing on Thanksgiving Eve," "In the North Woods," "In the Wee Hours," "Metamorphosis at Midnight," "On the Way to September," "Post Office Beneficence," "Season of Snow and Milk," "Swimming to Alaska," "Tourists of a Cold Apocalypse," "Village Mail Plane," and "The Weight of the Soul."

The following poems appeared in the chapbook *Praising Invisible Birds*, Finishing Line Press, 2008, "Conjuring Borealis," "Indiana, Late August," "Lady Astronomer," "Feeding an Orphan Reindeer Fawn," "Mister Handstand Man," "Praising Invisible Birds," "Pulling Sky Home with our Hands," "Walking in the Quaker Wood," and "What the Dead Miss Most."

ABOUT THE AUTHOR

Doris Jean Lynch grew up with seven siblings in the suburbs of Philadelphia. "My love of nature came early, partially inspired by my need for quiet. At first, with my older brother and then with my younger sisters, I wandered the Pennsylvania woods and fields at the edge of the suburbs." Her father, an aeronautical engineer, shared a love of the night sky with his children.

She graduated from Penn State University and two years later followed her family to New Orleans. The long months of heat and humidity convinced her and her husband, Thom, to relocate to Alaska with their toddler, Kristen. "In our VW bug, we chose an extra-long route, first visiting the Pacific Northwest, then driving through British Columbia and the Yukon on the ALCAN highway." She swam every day until they crossed into Alaska. They headed to Nome, and six weeks later to the Inupiat village of Kivalina. They spent the school year above the arctic circle. They later resettled in Juneau where their son, Cody, was born.

After six years, they left for Berkeley and advanced degrees, then spent a year in Yogyakarta, Indonesia. They have since lived in Bloomington, Indiana.

Lynch has published hundreds of poems along with short stories and essays in literary magazines and anthologies. This year MediaJazz published her first collection of haibun, *Meteor*

Hound. Haibun is a hybrid form of prose and haiku. In 2008, Finishing Line Press published her poetry chapbook *Praising Invisible Birds.* She has won many awards, including fellowships from the Alaska Council on the Arts, the Indiana Arts Council, and the Chester H. Jones Foundation. Her haibun awards include three from the Genjuan International Haibun contest and three from the Haiku Society of America.

Lynch has worked as a librarian, college professor, book reviewer, social worker for the blind, cab driver, waitress and deli-girl. She loves to swim, hike, and travel. She states, "I feel strongly that we must work hard to save our climate, and the natural world that sustains us and all our fellow creatures."

BOOKS BY BOTTOM DOG PRESS

HARMONY SERIES

Swimming to Alaska: Poems, by Doris Jean Lynch, 102 pgs., $16
Hope as a Construction, by David Adams, 182 pgs., $18
Baltic Amber in a Chest: Poems, by Clarissa Jakobsons, 104 pgs., $16
Choices: Three Novellas by Annabel Thomas, 176 pgs., $18
Pottery Town Blues, by Karen Kotrba, 128 pgs., $16
The Pears: Poems, by Larry Smith, 66 pgs, $15
Cycling Through Columbine, by JRW Case, 258 pgs., $18
Without a Plea, by Jeff Gundy, 96 pgs, $16
Taking a Walk in My Animal Hat, by Charlene Fix, 90 pgs, $16
Earnest Occupations, by Richard Hague, 200 pgs, $18
Pieces: A Composite Novel, by Mary Ann McGuigan, 250 pgs, $18
Crows in the Jukebox: Poems, by Mike James, 106 pgs, $16
Portrait of the Artist as a Bingo Worker: A Memoir, by Lori Jakiela, 216 pgs, $18
The Thick of Thin: A Memoir, by Larry Smith, 238 pgs, $18
Cold Air Return: A Novel, by Patrick Lawrence O'Keeffe, 390 pgs, $20
Flesh and Stones: A Memoir, by Jan Shoemaker, 176 pgs, $18
Waiting to Begin: A Memoir, by Patricia O'Donnell, 166 pgs, $18
And Waking: Poems, by Kevin Casey, 80 pgs, $16
Both Shoes Off: Poems, by Jeanne Bryner, 112 pgs, $16
Abandoned Homeland: Poems, by Jeff Gundy, 96 pgs, $16
Stolen Child: A Novel, by Suzanne Kelly, 338 pgs, $18

Bottom Dog Press, Inc.
P.O. Box 425 /Huron, Ohio 44839
http://smithdocs.net

Books by Bottom Dog Press

Harmony Series

The Canary: A Novel, by Michael Loyd Gray, 196 pgs, $18
On the Flyleaf: Poems, by Herbert Woodward Martin, 106 pgs, $16
The Harmonist at Nightfall: Poems of Indiana, by Shari Wagner,
114 pgs, $16
Painting Bridges: A Novel, by Patricia Averbach, 234 pgs, $18
Ariadne & Other Poems, by Ingrid Swanberg, 120 pgs, $16
The Search for the Reason Why: New and Selected Poems, by Tom Kryss,
192 pgs, $16
Kenneth Patchen: Rebel Poet in America, by Larry Smith,
Revised 2nd Edition, 326 pgs, Cloth $28
Selected Correspondence of Kenneth Patchen,
Edited with introduction by Allen Frost, Paper $18/ Cloth $28
Awash with Roses: Collected Love Poems of Kenneth Patchen,
Eds. Laura Smith and Larry Smith
with introduction by Larry Smith, 200 pgs, $16
Breathing the West: Great Basin Poems, by Liane Ellison Norman,
96 pgs, $16
Maggot: A Novel, by Robert Flanagan, 262 pgs, $18
American Poet: A Novel, by Jeff Vande Zande, 200 pgs, $18
The Way-Back Room: Memoir of a Detroit Childhood, by Mary Minock, 216
pgs, $18

Bottom Dog Press, Inc.
P.O. Box 425 /Huron, Ohio 44839
http://smithdocs.net

www.ingramcontent.com/pod-product-compliance
Lightning Source LLC
Chambersburg PA
CBHW031144090426
42738CB00008B/1211